Biography

Emilia Perez

The Rise of Karla Sofia Gascón – A Story of Courage, Identity, and Redemption

Lindsey T. Gordon

COPYRIGHT

TABLE OF CONTENTS

INTRODUCTION

A Tale of Transformation and Triumph

The story of Karla Sofía Gascón is one of unyielding resilience, an inspiring journey from personal discovery to professional triumph that has redefined boundaries in the film industry. Her rise to prominence as the star of "Emilia Pérez" is not just a testament to her extraordinary talent but also a reflection of the courage it takes to live authentically in a world that often resists change. Gascón's life embodies the struggle to embrace one's true self, overcome societal prejudice, and achieve greatness against all odds.

Born in Madrid during the repressive years of Francisco Franco's dictatorship, Gascón's early life was marked by the silent burden of suppressing her identity. As a child, she understood that she was a girl, but the rigid societal norms of the time left no room for such expressions.

Her journey into adulthood was defined by a constant negotiation between the reality of who she was and the external expectations placed upon her. Despite these challenges, her passion for performance emerged as a beacon of hope, offering a glimpse of a future where she could transcend the limits imposed by her circumstances.

Moving to Mexico in 2009, Gascón quickly established herself as a celebrated figure in telenovelas, captivating audiences with her powerful portrayals. However, even as her star rose, her internal struggle deepened. For years, she lived with the fear that publicly embracing her identity would jeopardize her career.

The decision to transition in 2018 marked a turning point, not only for her personal well-being but also for the broader conversation about representation and authenticity in the entertainment industry. Supported by her family, including her wife and teenage daughter, Gascón faced the challenges of transitioning in the public eye with remarkable bravery.

It was against this backdrop that "Emilia Pérez" emerged as a groundbreaking project. Directed by acclaimed filmmaker Jacques Audiard, the movie tells the story of a Mexican drug lord who undergoes gender affirmation surgery to escape his past and embrace a new life. The character of Emilia Pérez is a powerful metaphor for redemption, transformation, and the courage to reinvent oneself. Gascón's portrayal of both the pre-transition Manitas and the post-transition Emilia is a masterclass in acting, showcasing her ability to inhabit complex, layered characters with nuance and depth.

The film's premiere at the Cannes Film Festival was a moment of vindication for Gascón. Her performance received widespread acclaim, earning her and her co-stars the Best Actress award. More importantly, it marked her arrival as a trailblazer in an industry that had long overlooked the contributions of trans actors. "Emilia Pérez" was not just a cinematic achievement; it was a cultural moment, one that challenged audiences to reconsider their assumptions about gender, identity, and redemption.

Beyond its artistic merits, "Emilia Pérez" represents a seismic shift in how trans stories are told on screen. By insisting on playing both versions of the character, Gascón ensured that the narrative remained authentic, rejecting the traditional practice of casting separate actors for pre- and post-transition roles. Her involvement extended beyond acting; she collaborated with Audiard to refine the script, ensuring that the film's portrayal of trans experiences was both accurate and respectful.

Gascón's journey, however, is not just about her personal transformation or her professional milestones. It is also a story of social impact. As a public figure, she has used her platform to advocate for acceptance and understanding, inspiring countless others to live their truths.

In interviews, she speaks candidly about the challenges she has faced, from media scrutiny to transphobia, and the importance of resilience in the face of adversity. Her openness has resonated deeply with audiences, particularly within the Latino community, where her story has sparked important conversations about identity and inclusion.

Today, Karla Sofía Gascón stands as a symbol of what is possible when talent meets courage. Her role in *Emilia Pérez* is not just a career milestone; it is a beacon of hope for a more inclusive future in cinema and beyond. This tale of transformation and triumph is a reminder that authenticity is not just a personal victory but a powerful tool for social change.

CHAPTER ONE

Beginnings in Madrid

Madrid in the 1970s and early 1980s was a city in transition. Emerging from the shadow of Francisco Franco's dictatorship, Spain was undergoing a cultural and political awakening. But for young Karla Sofía Gascón, born during the waning years of this authoritarian regime, the rigid societal norms of the era imposed strict expectations that left little room for self-expression, especially for someone grappling with a deeply personal understanding of gender identity.

This chapter explores the early years of Gascón's life, her first encounters with the world of performance, and her quiet resilience in the face of a society unwilling to accept those who deviated from its strict norms.

Childhood Dreams and Early Struggles

From an early age, Karla Sofía Gascón felt different. By the age of 4, she understood an essential truth about herself: she was a girl. Yet, the world around her refused to acknowledge this reality. Growing up in a conservative household in a deeply patriarchal society, young Karla's identity was met with confusion, silence, or outright rejection. At the time, discussions around gender identity were virtually nonexistent, leaving her with no language or framework to articulate what she knew to be true.

The weight of this disconnect pressed heavily on her. School was a particularly challenging environment, as the rigid gender roles imposed by the Francoist educational system reinforced feelings of isolation. Yet even in these constrained circumstances, she found solace in her vivid imagination. Stories, music, and the drama of everyday life captivated her, providing an escape from the stifling expectations of her community.

Madrid's cultural backdrop also began to subtly influence her dreams. Despite the oppressive atmosphere, Spain's capital remained a hub for the arts, with theater and cinema serving as beacons of creativity. These early experiences planted the seeds of a lifelong passion for performance. While other children played traditional games, Karla found joy in creating characters, mimicking actors, and imagining herself in roles that transcended the limits of her reality.

Navigating Gender Identity in an Oppressive Society

Navigating adolescence in Francoist Spain proved to be an exercise in survival. The dictatorship's rigid moral code dictated nearly every aspect of daily life, from how people dressed to whom they were allowed to love. For Karla, this meant concealing her identity to avoid ostracism or worse. She learned to adapt, carefully crafting a persona that adhered to societal expectations while privately nurturing the truth of who she was.

This dual existence took a toll. Every day was a balancing act, as she sought to conform outwardly while grappling with an internal sense of authenticity. Questions swirled in her mind: Could she ever live as her true self? Would there ever be a world where she could be accepted as she was?

Despite the challenges, Karla displayed remarkable resilience. She developed a keen ability to observe the world around her, noting the hypocrisies and contradictions of those who enforced the status quo. This observational skill would later become a defining trait of her acting, allowing her to bring depth and authenticity to the characters she portrayed.

Social expectations dictated that young boys should excel in traditionally masculine pursuits, but Karla found herself drawn to the arts. Music, literature, and the vibrant characters she saw on screen offered a refuge. She admired strong, independent women in films, imagining herself as one of them—a vision of empowerment and freedom that sustained her through the most challenging years.

First Steps Toward Acting

Amidst the restrictions of her youth, performance emerged as a lifeline. Karla discovered early on that acting was not just an art form but a means of escape—a way to step into roles that allowed her to express emotions and experiences she could not otherwise share. Whether through school plays or informal performances for family and friends, she found that the stage offered a freedom she rarely experienced elsewhere.

Her fascination with acting deepened as she entered her teenage years. Films from around the world exposed her to characters and stories that mirrored her own struggles, albeit indirectly. She began to see acting not just as entertainment but as a powerful medium for exploring identity and human complexity. The art form became a bridge between the world she inhabited and the one she longed to create.

However, pursuing acting as a career in post-dictatorship Spain was no simple task. For one, the film and theater industries were dominated by traditional gender norms and often excluded those who did not fit into neatly defined roles. Undeterred, Karla began to develop her craft, studying performances and mimicking the gestures, expressions, and emotions of her favorite actors. She absorbed the nuances of their work, determined to one day bring her own voice to the stage and screen.

By the time she reached adulthood, Karla Sofía Gascón had not only honed her acting skills but also cultivated a deep well of emotional resilience. These early years, marked by quiet struggle and unshakable determination, laid the foundation for her future success. They also instilled in her a profound empathy—a quality that would later define her most memorable performances.

In many ways, acting was Karla's first step toward self-liberation. While society demanded that she conform, the stage allowed her to explore the possibilities of who she could be. This tension between public expectation and private authenticity would remain a recurring theme throughout her life and career, culminating in her transformative work in "Emilia Pérez."

Overall, as Madrid began to embrace its cultural renaissance in the post-Franco years, so too did Karla begin to envision a future where she could break free from societal constraints. The path ahead was uncertain, but one thing was clear: her journey as a performer—and as her true self—had only just begun.

CHAPTER TWO

Crossing Borders – A Move to Mexico

Karla Sofía Gascón's journey to self-discovery and professional success took a pivotal turn in 2009 when she decided to leave Spain for Mexico. It was a leap of faith, fueled by her desire for greater artistic opportunities and a fresh start in a country renowned for its rich film and television heritage.

This chapter delves into the motivations behind her move, her ascent in the competitive world of Mexican telenovelas, and the personal and professional challenges she overcame in a new cultural landscape.

Leaving Spain Behind

Spain in the early 2000s was undergoing significant social and cultural change, but for Karla, the environment remained stifling. Despite her burgeoning acting career, the opportunities available were limited, particularly for someone grappling with a concealed identity.

The Spanish entertainment industry, while vibrant, often adhered to rigid norms, leaving little room for deviation from the mainstream. For Karla, this translated into roles that felt confining and a professional landscape that mirrored the personal constraints she was working to overcome.

The decision to move to Mexico was both a professional and personal choice. Known for its robust entertainment industry, Mexico had long been a hub for telenovelas—dramatic television series that reached audiences across Latin America and beyond. The country's thriving arts scene offered an alluring prospect: a chance to reinvent herself and pursue the challenging, dynamic roles she craved.

Leaving behind her homeland was not an easy decision. Madrid had been her home, a place where she had forged early connections and begun to establish herself as an actress. But the promise of Mexico—a country that blended cultural richness with boundless creative potential—proved too enticing to resist. With a mix of hope and trepidation, she packed her bags and embarked on a new chapter.

Success in Telenovelas

The move to Mexico marked a turning point in Karla's career. She quickly discovered that the Mexican television industry, while competitive, was also a land of opportunity for those with talent and determination. With her striking presence, natural charisma, and a deep understanding of character work, she began to make waves in the world of telenovelas.

Her breakout role came in the critically acclaimed "Wild Heart" (Corazón Salvaje), a historical romance series that became a cultural phenomenon. The show, known for its sweeping storylines and larger-than-life characters, was a perfect fit for Karla's dramatic sensibilities. Her performance captivated audiences and earned her widespread recognition, catapulting her into the ranks of telenovela royalty.

Telenovelas became a proving ground for Karla's talents, allowing her to showcase her range and versatility. Whether playing a cunning antagonist or a sympathetic heroine, she brought depth and authenticity to her roles, quickly becoming a fan favorite. Her ability to inhabit complex characters resonated with viewers, who appreciated her commitment to her craft.

The success of her work in Mexican television also had a transformative impact on her career. No longer constrained by the limitations she had faced in Spain, Karla found herself part of an industry that valued her contributions and offered her a platform to grow. The acclaim she received opened doors to new projects, collaborations, and creative opportunities that she had only dreamed of in her earlier years.

Cultural Challenges and Triumphs

Relocating to a new country, however, came with its own set of challenges. Mexico's vibrant culture was vastly different from the one Karla had left behind in Spain, and adapting to her new environment required both resilience and flexibility. As a foreigner, she had to navigate unfamiliar social dynamics and establish herself in an industry where she was initially an outsider.

Language, despite being shared between Spain and Mexico, presented its own hurdles. The regional dialects, idioms, and cultural references were distinct, requiring Karla to immerse herself deeply in Mexican society to understand and reflect its nuances in her work. She threw herself into learning about her new home, embracing its traditions, history, and values. This cultural sensitivity not only endeared her to her colleagues and audiences but also enriched her performances, allowing her to bring authenticity to the Mexican characters she portrayed.

On a personal level, the move to Mexico represented a fresh start—a chance to explore her identity and make strides toward self-acceptance. Although she had not yet publicly transitioned, the physical and emotional distance from Spain gave her space to reflect on her journey and consider what living authentically might look like. In many ways, Mexico became both a professional and personal sanctuary, a place where she could begin to envision a future in which her career and identity could coexist.

Her success in telenovelas also brought visibility and influence. As she rose to fame, she became a symbol of perseverance and artistry, inspiring fans across Latin America and beyond. The accolades she received were not just a testament to her acting skills but also a reflection of her ability to connect with audiences on a deeply emotional level.

Despite the cultural and professional challenges she faced, Karla Sofía Gascón emerged from this period stronger and more determined than ever. Mexico had become more than just a destination; it was a crucible for growth, creativity, and self-discovery. The triumphs she achieved during these years laid the groundwork for the groundbreaking success of *Emilia Pérez* and the global recognition that would follow.

Overall, this chapter illustrates how Karla Sofía Gascón's move to Mexico was a pivotal moment in her life, both personally and professionally. It highlights her ability to adapt, thrive, and leave an indelible mark on an industry that became her second home. More importantly, it sets the stage for the transformative years ahead, as she continues to push boundaries, embrace her truth, and redefine what it means to succeed on one's own terms.

CHAPTER THREE

A Life in Shadows

While Karla Sofía Gascón's professional star was rising, her personal life was marked by an internal struggle that cast a long shadow over her achievements. Living as her authentic self remained an elusive goal, constrained by societal expectations and the fear of jeopardizing her career. This chapter explores her deeply personal battles with gender identity, the delicate balance of honesty in romantic relationships, and her darkest moments at the brink of despair.

Personal Struggles with Gender Identity

From a young age, Karla knew her truth: she was a woman. But growing up in a world that offered little understanding or acceptance of gender diversity forced her to suppress this reality. Even as she achieved success in her acting career, this internal conflict persisted. The tension between her public persona and her private identity created a duality that was both exhausting and deeply isolating.

In the entertainment industry, image is everything, and Karla feared that revealing her true self would alienate audiences and blacklist her from future roles. For years, she lived with the painful contradiction of portraying glamorous, confident characters onscreen while privately grappling with feelings of disconnection and dysphoria. Each time she stepped into a role, she felt a bittersweet mix of liberation and frustration—liberation in escaping into a character and frustration in not being able to live as her true self in her personal life.

Adding to this struggle was the pressure of public scrutiny. As her fame grew, so did the spotlight on her personal life. The fear of being "found out" became a constant companion, amplifying her anxiety and making her feel trapped. While her acting talent brought her accolades and admiration, it also served as a barrier to authenticity, as she worried that revealing her identity could unravel everything she had worked so hard to achieve.

For years, Karla's gender identity remained a private battle. Yet, even in the darkest moments of doubt and self-denial, there was a spark of resilience—a belief that someday, she could align her inner truth with her outward life. That hope, however fragile, sustained her through years of uncertainty.

Romantic Relationships and Honesty

Amid her personal struggles, Karla sought connection and companionship through romantic relationships. Love, she believed, could offer a reprieve from the loneliness of living inauthentically. However, navigating these relationships was far from simple. In an era and society where gender norms were rigidly enforced, being open about her identity with partners carried significant risks.

Remarkably, Karla chose honesty as her guiding principle in matters of the heart.

She made it a point to disclose her reality to the women she became romantically involved with, ensuring that they understood who she truly was. "All the women that have been with me knew the reality," she later explained. "I never deceived anyone." This honesty was a courageous act in a world where many others in her position might have felt compelled to hide.

Yet, honesty did not always shield her from pain. Some relationships ended because of her identity, a reminder of how deeply ingrained societal prejudices could be. Each rejection reinforced the fear that her truth might alienate not just lovers but also the broader world around her. Despite this, Karla remained resolute in her commitment to transparency, refusing to compromise her integrity for the sake of convenience or acceptance.

Her romantic relationships were not without moments of deep connection and support. The women who chose to stand by her offered love and understanding that helped sustain her through difficult times. Still, the societal pressures and personal insecurities surrounding her gender identity often cast a shadow over even her happiest moments, leaving her yearning for a world where she could love and be loved without fear or reservation.

At the Brink of Despair

As the years wore on, the weight of living a double life began to take a heavy toll on

Karla's mental health. The constant tension between her public image and private identity left her feeling trapped and hopeless. Despite her success in acting, she struggled to find joy in her achievements, as the specter of inauthenticity loomed over every triumph.

At her lowest point, Karla found herself confronting suicidal thoughts. The despair of believing she would never be able to live as her true self, coupled with the fear of losing her beloved acting career, seemed insurmountable. “I was at the border of suicide,” she later revealed. “I always thought I was going to have to give up this work that I love and that I would end up on the streets.”

These thoughts were compounded by the relentless pressure of societal expectations. The idea of transitioning—of aligning her physical self with her inner identity—felt both essential and impossible. Transitioning could mean freedom, but it also carried the risk of ostracism and professional ruin. For someone whose life was so deeply intertwined with her career, this risk felt unbearable.

Karla's strength during this time came from an unshakable determination to survive. She knew that giving up would mean surrendering not just her career but also the possibility of ever living authentically. This inner resolve, coupled with the support of loved ones, eventually pulled her back from the brink. She began to envision a future where she could reconcile her identity with her passion for acting, even if that path seemed fraught with uncertainty.

Overall, this chapter captures the raw, unfiltered reality of Karla Sofía Gascón's life during her years of internal struggle. It is a testament to her resilience and courage, illustrating the immense challenges she faced as she worked to reconcile her identity with her aspirations. The shadows that defined this period of her life would later serve as a source of strength, fueling her journey toward self-acceptance and paving the way for the transformative moments to come.

CHAPTER FOUR

Transitioning to Authenticity

The year 2018 marked a profound turning point in Karla Sofía Gascón's life: the moment she decided to transition and publicly embrace her identity as a transgender woman. It was a journey fraught with challenges, but also one defined by immense courage and the support of her family. This chapter explores the pivotal decision to transition, the intense media scrutiny she endured, and the vital role her family played in helping her navigate this transformative period.

Making the Decision

By 2018, Karla had spent decades wrestling with her identity, the emotional toll of living inauthentically, and the fear of losing her career. Despite her accomplishments in acting, the shadow of unfulfilled authenticity persisted. It was during this year that she finally decided to confront these fears head-on and begin the process of transitioning.

Karla's decision to transition was not made lightly. It was the culmination of years of introspection and self-discovery, as well as a recognition that continuing to suppress her identity was no longer sustainable. "I always knew who I was," she explained, "but the time had to be right." At age 46, she had reached a point where the cost of hiding her truth outweighed the risks of living authentically.

What made 2018 the right moment for her transition? For Karla, it was a confluence of factors. She felt a growing confidence in her ability to navigate the psychological and medical aspects of transitioning, thanks to the increasing availability of supportive healthcare professionals. Additionally, she began to see glimmers of societal change, with conversations around gender identity becoming more visible in global media and entertainment.

Equally important was her personal resolve. Karla had endured years of internal conflict, public scrutiny, and professional uncertainty. By the time she made the decision to transition, she had developed a resilience that would carry her through the challenges ahead. “I knew I had to do this,” she later reflected. "Not just for myself, but for everyone who might be inspired by my journey."

Facing Media Scrutiny

Karla's transition was not without its obstacles, and chief among them was the reaction of the media. As a well-known figure in Mexico and Spain, her decision to transition became a highly publicized story, with sensationalist headlines dominating the news cycle. While some outlets approached her story with sensitivity, others focused on shock value, often resorting to misgendering and deadnaming her.

The scrutiny was relentless. Mexican and Spanish tabloids dissected every aspect of her life, often framing her transition as a scandal rather than a personal milestone. Paparazzi followed her to public events, and commentators debated her decision with little regard for her privacy or humanity. “There are people who take joy in destroying other people’s lives,” Karla noted. “But they found their match with me. I’m a warrior.”

Despite the negativity, Karla remained steadfast in her commitment to live authentically. She used the media attention as an opportunity to educate the public about transgender issues, refusing to let the narrative be defined by ignorance or sensationalism. Her interviews became platforms for advocacy, as she spoke candidly about her journey and the importance of acceptance.

While the media scrutiny was undoubtedly challenging, it also underscored the courage of Karla's decision. By standing her ground in the face of criticism, she became a symbol of resilience and empowerment for others in the transgender community. Her ability to weather this storm demonstrated her strength and further cemented her status as a trailblazer.

Family as a Pillar of Strength

Amid the external challenges, Karla found unwavering support from the people who mattered most: her wife and teenage daughter. Their acceptance and encouragement were instrumental in helping her navigate the complexities of transitioning while maintaining her personal and professional equilibrium.

Karla's relationship with her wife was built on a foundation of honesty and mutual respect. From the beginning of their marriage, Karla had been open about her identity, ensuring there were no secrets between them. This transparency fostered a deep bond that remained strong even as their relationship evolved. "My wife stood by me every step of the way," Karla shared. "She gave me the strength to keep going, even when things were hard."

Her teenage daughter, too, played a vital role in her journey. Their relationship was marked by a unique blend of love, understanding, and camaraderie. As Karla transitioned, her daughter offered both emotional support and practical assistance, helping her navigate the challenges of a world that often refused to understand. The closeness between them was evident in their shared moments of joy, from bonding over fashion to finding solace in each other's presence.

For Karla, her family's support was a source of profound gratitude and inspiration. In a world that often felt hostile, they provided a safe haven where she could be herself without fear of judgment. Their belief in her reinforced her own sense of self-worth and gave her the courage to face the public with confidence.

Her family's support also carried a broader significance. In sharing their story, Karla highlighted the importance of acceptance and love within families. She hoped her example would inspire other parents to support their transgender children, emphasizing that unconditional love can make all the difference.

Karla Sofía Gascón's transition to authenticity was not just a personal transformation but a public act of courage. It required her to confront societal prejudices, endure invasive media attention, and navigate the complexities of redefining her public image. Yet, through it all, she remained true to herself, drawing strength from her family and an unwavering belief in the power of authenticity.

Overall, this chapter captures the resilience and determination that defined this pivotal period in Karla's life. It also sets the stage for her next chapter, as she began to embrace her newfound identity with pride and channel her experiences into her art, paving the way for her groundbreaking work in “Emilia Pérez.”

CHAPTER FIVE

The Birth of Emilia Pérez

The creation of "Emilia Pérez" was a landmark moment in Karla Sofía Gascón's career, blending the visionary direction of Jacques Audiard with her own transformative performance. The film emerged as a bold narrative that combined themes of redemption, identity, and resilience, mirroring Karla's personal journey in profound ways.

This chapter explores the origins of the project, the unique challenges of her dual role, and the deeply personal resonance of the story.

The Vision of Jacques Audiard

Jacques Audiard, the celebrated French writer and director, is known for crafting films that delve into complex human emotions and relationships. With "Emilia Pérez," he sought to tell a story unlike any he had told before—a musical drama that would challenge societal perceptions and provide a platform for underrepresented voices. At the heart of this narrative was the character of Manitas, a ruthless Mexican drug lord who transitions into Emilia Pérez, a woman seeking redemption for her violent past.

From the outset, Audiard knew that authenticity was crucial to the success of the project. He envisioned a trans actress in the role, believing that only someone with lived experience could bring the necessary depth and truth to the character. "Casting Karla Sofía Gascón was essential," Audiard explained. "Her insight, her strength, and her personal story elevated this film beyond what I could have imagined."

Audiard's vision extended beyond casting. He wanted "Emilia Pérez" to challenge stereotypes and offer a nuanced exploration of gender, identity, and transformation. To achieve this, he worked closely with Karla, seeking her input on the script and her perspective on the character. "Karla was my teacher," Audiard later shared. "She guided me in understanding what was authentic and what needed to be changed. Her voice shaped this film as much as mine."

The collaboration between Audiard and Karla was a testament to mutual respect and shared artistry. Together, they crafted a story that was both groundbreaking and deeply personal, setting the stage for a performance that would redefine cinematic storytelling.

A Role Unlike Any Other

For Karla Sofía Gascón, the role of Manitas/Emilia was both a challenge and an honor. As an actress, she had always sought roles that allowed her to push boundaries and explore new dimensions of her craft. But playing two versions of the same character—a fearsome kingpin and the woman he becomes—was a task that required unparalleled emotional and physical commitment.

Initially, Audiard had considered casting two actors to portray Manitas and Emilia, but Karla insisted on playing both roles. "I don't want others to do my part!" she joked during interviews. Beyond the humor, her determination stemmed from a belief in her own abilities and a desire to showcase the transformative power of acting. "I'm an actress," she explained. "And I want to do roles that are as far away from me as possible."

To portray Manitas, Karla delved into the psyche of a character defined by violence and power. She studied the mannerisms, speech patterns, and emotional detachment of real-life drug lords, crafting a persona that was both terrifying and magnetic. Transitioning into Emilia required a complete shift, as the character embraced vulnerability and sought atonement for her past. For Karla, this duality was the essence of the story—a reflection of the capacity for change and growth within every individual.

The physical demands of the role were equally challenging. From dramatic costume changes to the intricacies of musical numbers, Karla brought a level of dedication that impressed both the cast and crew. Her performance was hailed as transformative, with critics praising her ability to seamlessly embody two distinct yet connected identities. For Karla, the experience was deeply rewarding. "This role allowed me to explore parts of myself I had never touched before," she shared. "It was a journey of discovery, both as an actress and as a person."

Themes of Redemption and Resilience

At its core, "Emilia Pérez" is a story of redemption—a theme that resonated deeply with Karla Sofía Gascón. The film follows Emilia as she attempts to make amends for the violence and destruction caused by her past life as Manitas. Through acts of charity and a commitment to helping victims of cartel violence, Emilia seeks to redefine herself and find peace.

For Karla, the parallels between the character's journey and her own were striking. Like Emilia, she had faced judgment and prejudice, as well as the challenge of rebuilding her life on her own terms. The themes of resilience and transformation mirrored her personal experiences, adding a layer of authenticity to her performance. "I understood Emilia because I had lived some of her struggles," Karla explained. "Her desire for redemption, her fight to be seen for who she truly is—these are battles I know well."

The film also explored broader questions of identity and acceptance, challenging audiences to reconsider their perceptions of gender and transformation. Emilia's journey was not just about atoning for her past but also about embracing her present and future. It was a narrative of hope and possibility, offering a powerful message about the capacity for change within us all.

Working on "Emilia Pérez" gave Karla a platform to highlight these themes on a global stage. She viewed the film as more than just a career milestone; it was an opportunity to spark dialogue and inspire others. "This story is about more than one person," she emphasized. "It's about all of us—the mistakes we make, the ways we hurt each other, and the ways we can heal."

Overall, the birth of "Emilia Pérez" was a transformative moment for Karla Sofía Gascón. It allowed her to channel her experiences into a performance that was both groundbreaking and deeply personal. Through her collaboration with Jacques Audiard and her portrayal of a character that spanned two identities, Karla not only elevated her craft but also contributed to a story that challenged conventions and celebrated resilience. This chapter marks a pivotal point in her journey, setting the stage for the critical acclaim and cultural impact that would follow.

CHAPTER SIX

Cannes and Critical Acclaim

The debut of "Emilia Pérez" at the Cannes Film Festival was a defining moment for both Karla Sofía Gascón and the film itself. The standing ovation, critical acclaim, and shared Best Actress award marked a turning point in her career, proving that stories about transformation and redemption could move global audiences.

Yet, even amidst this triumph, Karla faced the challenges of navigating an industry still grappling with bias and prejudice. This chapter explores the film's historic reception, the duality of praise and resistance, and the profound connection it fostered with audiences worldwide.

A Standing Ovation at Cannes

When "Emilia Pérez" premiered at Cannes in May, it was met with overwhelming acclaim. The audience response was immediate and powerful, culminating in a ten-minute standing ovation that left the cast and crew visibly moved. For Karla Sofía Gascón, standing on that prestigious stage was a moment of validation—not just for her performance but for her journey as an actress and a woman.

The Cannes audience praised the film's bold storytelling, its unapologetic celebration of identity, and its seamless blending of drama and music. Critics lauded Karla's performance as transformative, highlighting her ability to embody two distinct facets of the same character with authenticity and depth. Alongside her co-stars Zoe Saldana, Selena Gomez, and Adriana Paz, Karla was awarded the shared Best Actress prize—a historic achievement that placed her in the international spotlight.

Accepting the award was an emotional experience for Karla. "This is not just a win for me," she said in her acceptance speech. "It is a win for everyone who has ever felt unseen, misunderstood, or judged. It is proof that our stories matter and that our voices deserve to be heard." Her words resonated with many, reflecting the broader significance of her achievement as a trans actress breaking barriers in a traditionally conservative industry.

The Cannes premiere set the stage for "Emilia Pérez" to become an awards season favorite, with critics predicting Oscar nominations and further accolades. For Karla, however, the real victory was the opportunity to connect with audiences on a deeply personal level.

Overcoming Industry Bias

While the critical acclaim for "Emilia Pérez" was undeniable, the road to recognition was not without its obstacles. As a trans actress in a lead role, Karla faced both overt and subtle biases from an industry that has historically marginalized transgender performers. Even amidst the praise, there were moments of ignorance and prejudice that underscored the challenges of achieving true inclusivity in Hollywood.

One telling incident occurred during the film's awards campaign, when an industry insider asked Karla whether she would be nominated for Best Actress or Best Actor. The question, though perhaps unintentionally insensitive, revealed lingering misunderstandings about gender identity in the entertainment world. Karla handled the situation with grace, firmly asserting her identity. "I am an actress," she replied. "If I played a monster or an old dog, I would still be nominated as an actress."

This moment was emblematic of the larger barriers Karla has faced throughout her career. While she was lauded for her performance, there were those who questioned her legitimacy as a leading lady, perpetuating outdated notions of gender and talent. Yet, rather than allowing these biases to diminish her achievements, Karla used them as opportunities for education and advocacy. “Every conversation is a chance to open minds,” she said. “I don’t take it personally—I see it as part of the journey toward understanding.”

Karla’s resilience in the face of prejudice was a testament to her strength and determination. By standing her ground and embracing her role as both an actress and an advocate, she continued to challenge the industry to evolve, paving the way for future generations of transgender performers.

A Connection with Audiences

Beyond the accolades and industry recognition, what truly defined “Emilia

Pérez" was its ability to connect with audiences on a profound level. The film's themes of identity, redemption, and transformation resonated deeply with viewers from diverse backgrounds, sparking conversations about acceptance, forgiveness, and the power of change.

For many in the LGBTQ+ community, Karla's portrayal of Emilia was a source of inspiration and validation. Her performance captured the complexities of transitioning and the courage it takes to live authentically, offering a narrative that was both deeply personal and universally relatable. "Emilia's story is my story," one viewer wrote on social media. "It's about finding yourself, no matter how hard the journey."

The film's impact extended beyond LGBTQ+ audiences, touching anyone who had ever grappled with questions of identity or sought redemption for past mistakes. Emilia's transformation from a feared kingpin to a compassionate advocate was a testament to the human capacity for growth and change, a message that resonated across cultural and societal boundaries.

Karla's own journey added an additional layer of authenticity to the film. Viewers were moved not only by her performance but also by her courage in sharing her story with the world. Her openness about her struggles and triumphs inspired countless individuals to embrace their own truths, fostering a sense of solidarity and hope.

As "Emilia Pérez" continued to gain momentum on the global stage, it became clear that its greatest achievement was its ability to touch hearts and minds. For Karla, this connection with audiences was the ultimate reward. "The biggest prize for me," she said, "is the love and understanding I've felt from people around the world. That's what makes it all worth it."

Overall, the debut of "Emilia Pérez" at Cannes marked a watershed moment in Karla Sofía Gascón's career and the broader film industry. It was a celebration of artistry, resilience, and the power of storytelling to bridge divides and foster empathy. Yet, the journey was far from over, as Karla prepared to navigate the challenges and opportunities that lay ahead.

This chapter captures the triumph and complexity of this pivotal moment, setting the stage for her continued rise as a trailblazing actress and advocate.

CHAPTER SEVEN

Challenges on the Oscar Trail

As "Emilia Pérez" gained momentum on the awards circuit, Karla Sofía Gascón found herself navigating an entirely new terrain: the high-stakes and often grueling process of an Oscar campaign. While the film's critical acclaim and her groundbreaking performance positioned her as a strong contender for a Best Actress nomination, the journey was marked by both triumph and adversity.

This chapter explores the significance of her campaign, the moments of ignorance she faced, and the broader impact of her potential recognition on the LGBTQ+ community and aspiring actors.

Campaigning for Representation

A potential Best Actress nomination for Karla Sofía Gascón would not just be a personal milestone—it would be a historic achievement for transgender representation in Hollywood. If nominated, Karla would become the first trans woman recognized in this category, marking a momentous step forward for an industry that has often overlooked or marginalized transgender talent.

For Karla, the weight of this possibility was not lost. "It would be absolutely wonderful and a real source of pride," she acknowledged. "But honestly, if it doesn't happen, it's not a big deal. The biggest prize for me has been the connection I've felt with the audience." Her grounded perspective underscored her focus on the larger implications of her work rather than individual accolades.

Campaigning for an Oscar involves extensive press tours, interviews, and events designed to keep a film and its performers in the public eye. For Karla, this process was an opportunity to amplify the importance of authentic representation. In interviews, she spoke candidly about the barriers faced by transgender actors and emphasized the need for Hollywood to embrace diverse stories and talent.

Her potential nomination sparked conversations across the entertainment industry about the evolving landscape of awards recognition. Many critics highlighted the importance of acknowledging performances that challenged societal norms and celebrated individuality. "This is not just about one actress or one film," wrote one prominent awards columnist. "It's about an industry finally beginning to reflect the world as it truly is."

While Karla remained humble about her chances, her campaign was a rallying cry for greater inclusivity and visibility, reminding audiences and voters alike that representation on the biggest stage matters.

Facing Ignorance and Misunderstanding

Despite the progress represented by her campaign, Karla encountered moments of ignorance and prejudice that revealed the work still needed to achieve true acceptance. One particularly jarring instance occurred when an industry figure asked her whether she would be considered for Best Actress or Best Actor. The question, though perhaps unintentional in its insensitivity, reflected a lack of understanding about gender identity and reinforced the challenges trans performers face even in moments of success.

Karla's response was both firm and eloquent. "I am an actress," she stated unequivocally. "If I played a monster or an old dog, I would still be nominated as an actress." Her ability to address such moments with grace and humor not only defused tension but also served as a teaching moment for those unfamiliar with the realities of being a trans actor.

Beyond individual interactions, Karla also faced broader resistance from certain segments of the industry and the public. Social media, while a platform for support, was also a space where she encountered transphobic comments and attempts to undermine her achievements. Some critics dismissed her campaign as a "political statement" rather than a recognition of her talent, perpetuating harmful stereotypes about diversity in the arts.

Karla's resilience in the face of these challenges was a testament to her strength and commitment to her craft. "There will always be people who try to tear others down," she reflected. "But they don't define me or my work. My focus is on the people who see themselves in my story and find hope in it."

By confronting ignorance head-on and remaining steadfast in her identity, Karla turned obstacles into opportunities for education and dialogue, further solidifying her role as a trailblazer in the industry.

Becoming a Symbol of Hope

For aspiring actors in the LGBTQ+ community, Karla Sofía Gascón's recognition on the awards trail was far more than a personal achievement—it was a beacon of hope. Her journey from a life lived in shadows to international acclaim represented the possibilities that could emerge when authenticity and talent were allowed to shine.

Karla's openness about her struggles and triumphs resonated deeply with those who had faced similar challenges. Young transgender actors, in particular, found inspiration in her story, seeing her success as proof that their dreams were achievable despite societal barriers. "She gives me hope that one day, I can be myself and still pursue my passion," wrote one aspiring performer on social media.

Her impact extended beyond the entertainment industry, touching anyone who had ever felt marginalized or misunderstood. Through her interviews and public appearances, Karla emphasized the importance of embracing one's identity and pursuing one's goals without compromise. "Whether someone is a bus driver, a teacher, or an astronaut, what does it matter who they are as long as they do their job well?" she said.

Karla's visibility also challenged stereotypes and expanded perceptions of what transgender actors could achieve. By excelling in a role that required her to embody both a feared drug lord and a compassionate advocate, she demonstrated the range and depth of her talent, shattering preconceived notions about gender and performance.

As the Oscar race continued, Karla remained focused on her ultimate goal: using her platform to create a more inclusive and accepting world. "If my work can inspire even one person to embrace who they are, then it's all worth it," she said. "I hope that families will take their daughters and sons as they come, show them love, and say, 'Why not?'"

Overall, this chapter captures the complexity of Karla Sofía Gascón's journey on the Oscar trail, highlighting the triumphs and challenges of advocating for representation in a changing industry. Through her grace, resilience, and talent,

Karla not only positioned herself as a leading contender but also as a symbol of hope for countless individuals who saw their own struggles and aspirations reflected in her story.

CHAPTER EIGHT

Beyond Acting – Advocacy and Education

Karla Sofía Gascón's journey as an actor has not only reshaped the trajectory of her career but has also given her a platform to advocate for the rights and visibility of transgender individuals. Beyond her critically acclaimed role in "Emilia Pérez" and the possibility of making history with an Oscar nomination, Gascón has emerged as a powerful voice for change.

This chapter delves into how she uses her visibility to educate others, the importance of allies in the fight for understanding, and how she aims to plant the seeds of acceptance and diversity within families, communities, and industries.

Educating Through Visibility

In a world where trans representation in mainstream media has often been either sparse or misrepresented, Karla Sofía Gascón's visibility is a beacon of education and progress. For Karla, acting is more than just a career—it is a tool through which she can inform and inspire. Every interview, public appearance, and on-screen performance provides an opportunity to educate viewers about the lived experiences of transgender people.

One of the most profound ways Gascón educates is through her authenticity. Her openness about her personal journey—from childhood struggles with identity to the decision to transition—offers a rare and unfiltered look at what it means to be a trans person in the world today. “The best I can hope for is that people identify with who I am and what I’m doing, and they can see that it’s normal,” she shared in one interview. “I just want to show that I am no different than anybody else.”

Her performance in “Emilia Pérez” is another vehicle for this education. By playing a trans woman who takes on a leadership role within a violent cartel, Karla shatters the traditional molds of both gender and power. She doesn’t just play a trans character—she plays a complex, multi-dimensional human being, someone whose redemption and humanity resonate far beyond her gender. This powerful portrayal challenges audiences to rethink their assumptions about trans identities and the capacity for growth and change.

Through her visibility, Karla also addresses the misconceptions and stereotypes that often surround transgender people. By showing herself as an accomplished actress, a loving wife, and a devoted mother, she presents a narrative where gender is only one facet of her identity—allowing others to see the full richness of her humanity.

By educating others through her work and public persona, Karla Sofía Gascón ensures that transgender voices and stories are no longer sidelined but are integral to the broader societal dialogue about equality, inclusion, and human rights.

The Role of Allies

While Karla's advocacy is undoubtedly vital, she acknowledges that allies play an essential role in creating lasting change. One of the most significant and visible examples of allyship in her journey is the support she has received from co-stars like Selena Gomez. Their friendship and collaboration on "Emilia Pérez" serve as a model of solidarity, showing how important it is for people from different backgrounds to stand together and amplify marginalized voices.

Selena Gomez has been an outspoken ally to Karla, offering not just professional support but also personal encouragement. The bond between them extends beyond the set, with Karla noting that the two have become close friends and that their daughters share a special connection. “Sometimes they share shoes because they’re the same size!” Karla jokes, underscoring the joy and kinship that has developed between their families.

Such personal connections are crucial in breaking down barriers of misunderstanding. Allies like Gomez use their platforms to champion trans representation, ensuring that the visibility Karla brings is not limited to her own narrative but extends to the broader need for inclusivity in the entertainment industry.

Allies also serve as key educators themselves, showing that trans issues are not solely the responsibility of transgender people to explain. When Gomez speaks out in support of Karla, she contributes to creating a ripple effect of awareness and acceptance that touches her massive fan base. By standing with Karla, Gomez helps normalize the inclusion of trans narratives, creating spaces for more diverse voices to be heard in Hollywood.

Beyond individual allies, the support of the broader community—including industry professionals, filmmakers, and audience members—helps to foster a culture of understanding and respect. Gascón's work has been met with overwhelming praise, and the growing support from her co-stars, fellow actors, and the industry at large speaks volumes about the positive influence of allies in breaking down long-standing prejudices.

Planting Seeds for Change

Karla Sofía Gascón's influence stretches beyond her individual career; she is committed to planting the seeds for long-term societal change. Whether through her work in the entertainment industry or her advocacy in public spaces, Karla is passionate about encouraging acceptance, diversity, and love, starting with families and extending to larger societal structures.

For Karla, the home is one of the most important spaces for cultivating change. She has often spoken about the vital role of families in shaping inclusive attitudes, especially toward gender and sexuality. "I hope that families will take their daughters and sons as they come, show them love, and say, 'Why not?'" she said. She believes that if children are raised in environments that foster empathy and acceptance of differences, they will grow up with a broader understanding of the world, and this will translate into a more inclusive future.

Karla's message is clear: gender should not define or limit someone's potential. She advocates for a world where individuals are accepted for who they are, without fear of discrimination or prejudice. She envisions a future where a person's profession, passion, or dreams are never dictated by their gender, and where diversity is celebrated rather than feared.

In this light, her activism extends beyond public appearances and speeches—it is embedded in the work she does in front of the camera and the way she carries herself in the world. Through her actions, Karla shows that gender, like any other aspect of a person's identity, should be respected but never used to limit what someone can accomplish.

Karla also calls for greater inclusivity in industries beyond entertainment. In every conversation, whether in interviews or speeches, she encourages businesses, governments, and educational systems to prioritize diversity in hiring, policy-making, and everyday practices. She believes that true change requires action across all sectors of society, from healthcare to education to corporate leadership. "What matters most," Karla says, "is that we all have the right to live authentically, no matter where we are or what we do."

As Karla continues her work as both an actor and advocate, her ultimate goal is to see a world where being different is not just accepted, but celebrated. Her belief in planting the seeds for change is rooted in her personal experiences and her unwavering dedication to using her platform for good. By sharing her story, championing visibility, and fostering allyship, Karla Sofía Gascón is sowing the foundation for a more inclusive future, one where acceptance, love, and diversity reign.

Overall, this chapter illustrates the deeper layers of Karla Sofía Gascón's impact on society. Beyond her incredible career achievements, she remains dedicated to advocacy, visibility, and education. Through her work, she is changing the narrative about transgender identities, showing the world that true acceptance begins with understanding and respect.

Her influence, both on and off screen, will continue to inspire future generations to embrace their true selves and create a world where diversity is not just recognized but celebrated.

CHAPTER NINE

Dreams for the Future

As Karla Sofía Gascón continues to shape her legacy as an actress, advocate, and symbol of resilience, her dreams for the future go beyond the accolades and recognition she has already earned. While she has already defied the odds in the entertainment industry and broken barriers with her groundbreaking role in "Emilia Pérez," Gascón's aspirations extend toward new creative horizons, further impact on societal change, and a world where authentic self-expression is celebrated without limitations.

This chapter explores her ambitions to expand her craft, continue to bridge gaps across diverse communities, and her vision for a future where everyone is empowered to live freely as their true selves.

Expanding Her Craft

Karla Sofía Gascón has already demonstrated her formidable range as an actress through her role in *Emilia Pérez*, where she showcased not only her dramatic skills but also her ability to embody complex, multifaceted characters. However, Gascón is not one to be content with merely proving her talents—she is driven by a relentless desire to challenge herself, explore new genres, and take on roles that stretch her creative limits.

“I want to do everything,” she says with a spark of excitement. Her ambitions span across genres and roles, from comedy to action to even playing villainous characters. Gascón is particularly intrigued by the idea of playing roles that are completely different from anything she's done before. "I would love to play a James Bond villain who wants to destroy the world!" she says conspiratorially, laughing as she envisions herself in a larger-than-life role that contrasts with her previous portrayals.

Gascón is driven by the notion that great actors should not be confined by typecasting or preconceptions about what roles they can or cannot play. For her, the thrill of acting lies in the unpredictability and diversity of the roles she takes on. She understands the power of storytelling and its ability to challenge societal norms, which is why she is particularly eager to bring her unique perspective to genres that have traditionally lacked transgender representation.

Comedy, in particular, is an area that Karla is excited to explore. Comedy has long been an underrepresented genre for transgender performers, and Gascón sees it as an opportunity to break new ground. The idea of making people laugh, of bringing joy to others while subverting expectations, is deeply appealing to her. For her, comedy provides a new canvas to not only entertain but also to challenge the conventions surrounding gender and identity.

Additionally, Gascón has spoken about her desire to explore action films—roles that allow her to tap into a sense of power, authority, and physicality that she has not often been afforded as a trans woman in the industry. By stepping into action-packed roles, she seeks to demonstrate that women, especially trans women, can be formidable, strong, and capable of leading thrilling stories. This interest in action roles speaks to her desire to not only diversify her portfolio but also to redefine the limits of what it means to be a woman on screen.

Through these varied pursuits, Karla Sofía Gascón intends to continue pushing boundaries, not just for herself but for future generations of transgender performers who may not yet see themselves reflected in these diverse genres. Her drive to expand her craft is rooted in her deep belief that artistry knows no bounds—and that everyone, regardless of their identity, should have the opportunity to explore all facets of their creativity.

Building Bridges Across Communities

While Gascón has already had a transformative impact within the entertainment industry, she is also deeply committed to fostering greater unity across different communities—especially through the art of storytelling.

For Karla, stories have the power to connect people, break down walls of misunderstanding, and build empathy between groups that may otherwise remain isolated from one another. As an actress, she understands that the characters she portrays and the narratives she participates in can become powerful tools for social change.

Having experienced firsthand the transformative effect of representation, Karla is determined to use her platform to build bridges between various cultural, ethnic, and gender-diverse communities. Through her roles, interviews, and advocacy, she aims to unite people who may not traditionally have shared experiences but can find common ground in the stories she tells.

“Emilia Pérez,” for example, does not only speak to the trans community—it speaks to the universal themes of redemption, resilience, and the possibility of transformation. Karla's portrayal of Emilia transcends gender identity and touches on broader human experiences, such as the search for meaning, the burden of past actions, and the desire to atone. In this way, Gascón hopes to create a more inclusive world where different communities can see their own stories reflected on screen and understand the experiences of others.

Her advocacy also extends beyond the LGBTQ+ community to include marginalized voices of all kinds. Whether speaking out for women's rights, racial justice, or immigrant rights, Karla recognizes the intersectionality of oppression and the need for solidarity between groups. In her eyes, bridging these communities through storytelling is one of the most powerful ways to create meaningful change.

Moreover, Gascón views her work in entertainment as an opportunity to challenge systemic biases and reframe narratives around identity. As the entertainment industry increasingly embraces diverse voices and experiences, Gascón remains at the forefront of this change, using her visibility to promote greater inclusivity across all aspects of culture. Her passion for uniting communities through storytelling aligns with her broader mission to make the world a more accepting and empathetic place.

Living Authentically Without Barriers

At the heart of Karla Sofía Gascón's dreams for the future is her vision for a world where people are free to live authentically without the fear of judgment, discrimination, or limitation. Throughout her journey, she has confronted not only the external pressures of societal expectations but also the internal battles that come with navigating the complexities of identity. Despite the challenges, Karla has maintained an unwavering commitment to living her truth—and she hopes to inspire others to do the same.

"I just want to live my life without anybody bothering me," Karla has said. Her vision for the future is one where the barriers she faced—whether in her personal life or her professional career—no longer exist. In an ideal world, individuals would not have to fight for their right to be who they are. Instead, they would be celebrated and supported for embracing their true selves.

This vision extends to the entertainment industry, where Karla hopes to see more roles that allow actors to express themselves without being pigeonholed into stereotypes. In her ideal world, gender, race, and sexuality would be irrelevant factors in casting decisions—what would matter most would be the ability to act and connect with an audience. She wants a world where performers like her, and others from underrepresented backgrounds, are given the same opportunities to shine as anyone else, regardless of their identity.

Moreover, Karla hopes that as she continues to evolve as an artist, she will become a role model for those who may feel they cannot pursue their passions because of societal expectations. Her journey is one of perseverance and courage, and through her success, she hopes to demonstrate that anyone, regardless of background or identity, can thrive in their chosen field.

Karla's dream is not just a personal one—it is a vision for society as a whole. She wants to see a future where everyone has the freedom to express their identity without fear, where diversity is seen as a strength, and where barriers no longer exist between who someone is and who they can become. She is committed to planting the seeds for such a world through her work, her advocacy, and her unwavering dedication to living authentically.

Overall, as Karla Sofía Gascón moves forward in her career and her life, her dreams for the future remain rooted in a desire to create a more inclusive, accepting, and diverse world.

Through expanding her craft, building bridges across communities, and fighting for the right to live authentically, Gascón continues to break new ground—not just for herself but for others who may one day follow in her footsteps. Her legacy is not only one of artistic excellence but also one of social change, reminding us all that the future belongs to those who dare to live and love without barriers.

CHAPTER TEN

The Legacy of Karla Sofía Gascón

Karla Sofía Gascón's journey to stardom and her groundbreaking role in "Emilia Pérez" have solidified her place as a true trailblazer in the entertainment industry. As an actress, advocate, and symbol of resilience, Gascón has not only changed the narrative for transgender individuals in cinema but has also inspired countless others to pursue their dreams without fear of judgment or limitation.

Her legacy is defined by her ability to break barriers, empower future generations, and demonstrate the power of resilience, making her a beacon for others who follow in her footsteps. This chapter delves into the long-term impact of her work, how her story continues to inspire aspiring actors, and the resilience that has come to define her remarkable career and life.

Breaking Barriers in Cinema

Karla Sofía Gascón's role in "Emilia Pérez" represents more than just a career-defining moment for the actress; it is a milestone in the broader history of cinema. In an industry where transgender actors have long been underrepresented, Gascón's performance as both Manitas and Emilia not only brought visibility to the transgender experience but also showcased the immense talent and depth that transgender individuals can bring to complex roles.

"Emilia Pérez," with its powerful themes of redemption, transformation, and personal struggle, is a story that transcends gender. Yet it is undeniably a story of a trans woman who has gone through unimaginable challenges to reconcile her past and embrace a future as her authentic self.

The film broke new ground in the portrayal of a transgender character, offering an authentic, multifaceted representation rarely seen in mainstream cinema. The decision to cast Karla Sofía Gascón—an experienced trans actress—was crucial, as it ensured that the character's experiences were not only depicted accurately but also sensitively.

The impact of “Emilia Pérez” on the cinematic landscape is already evident. By showcasing a trans woman as the central figure of a major film, Gascón and the filmmakers defied expectations, challenging the industry’s long-standing tendency to marginalize or misrepresent transgender stories.

This film has already inspired other filmmakers to consider trans actors for leading roles, and its success at prestigious festivals like Cannes signals a promising future for more diverse and inclusive stories. The ripple effects of *Emilia Pérez* will be felt for years to come, reshaping the representation of gender and identity in film.

Moreover, Gascón's potential Oscar nomination for Best Actress is an achievement that goes far beyond her own career. If she succeeds in earning this nomination, it will mark a historic moment in the Academy's history, proving that transgender actors can excel in mainstream film and earn recognition in the highest echelons of the industry. Whether or not she wins, her candidacy is a testament to her remarkable talent and an acknowledgment of the importance of trans representation in Hollywood.

In the long run, Karla Sofía Gascón's role in "Emilia Pérez" will be remembered as a pivotal moment in cinema history—one that not only broke barriers but also inspired a new era of representation, inclusivity, and authenticity in storytelling.

Inspiring Future Generations

Karla Sofía Gascón's legacy extends far beyond her roles on screen. As a trailblazer and a vocal advocate for transgender rights and visibility, she has become a beacon of hope for aspiring trans actors and creators worldwide. Her story—of overcoming adversity, fighting for authenticity, and ultimately achieving success—resonates with individuals who may feel excluded from the entertainment industry due to their gender identity.

For many young trans individuals, Gascón represents what is possible when one refuses to be silenced or erased. Her journey—from growing up in a society that was not supportive of her gender identity to transitioning later in life and still achieving major success—proves that there is no timeline for success and no "right way" to pursue one's dreams. Her story serves as a reminder that self-acceptance and self-expression should never be postponed for fear of rejection.

As a mentor, Gascón has been open about her experiences and struggles, offering advice and guidance to aspiring trans artists. By sharing her journey, both the triumphs and the struggles, she has provided a roadmap for those who come after her. Her visibility in major international films like "Emilia Pérez" shows future generations that they do not have to compromise who they are to succeed in their chosen fields.

Karla's advocacy also focuses on the importance of building supportive networks within the industry. She speaks candidly about the value of having allies—like her co-stars in "Emilia Pérez," including Selena Gomez—who champion the work of marginalized individuals and help amplify their voices. This collaborative spirit is one that Gascón emphasizes as a crucial component of success, especially in an industry that has historically overlooked or undervalued trans talent.

Moreover, her role in "Emilia Pérez" serves as an essential piece of a larger conversation about diversity and inclusion. The groundbreaking nature of her performance has inspired more trans actors to pursue opportunities in mainstream cinema, where they previously may have felt overlooked. Gascón's ability to navigate Hollywood's complex and often exclusionary landscape has made her a role model for others—proving that with persistence, courage, and the right opportunities, a trans person can break into and thrive in an industry that has long been closed off to them.

Her visibility has already opened doors for other trans creatives in both front-of-house and behind-the-scenes roles, and her legacy will undoubtedly continue to encourage and inspire those who follow in her footsteps.

The Strength of a Warrior

Karla Sofía Gascón's resilience is perhaps her most defining characteristic. From a young age, she understood the power of inner strength and perseverance. Growing up in Madrid under the shadow of Franco's dictatorship, facing a society that rejected her identity, Gascón was forced to contend with both personal and external barriers. Despite the pain and struggles she faced, her indomitable will kept her pushing forward.

Her journey to authenticity was not easy—there were moments of despair, as she considered giving up on acting and even contemplated suicide. But Gascón's strength, which she describes as "warrior" energy, allowed her to persevere through some of the darkest times in her life. She had to fight not only for the right to exist as her true self but also for the right to do what she loved—act—and to be respected for her talent in an industry that was not always kind to her.

That warrior spirit has defined her both on and off the screen. Whether she is confronting ignorance or answering transphobic questions with grace and poise, Gascón has consistently exemplified what it means to stand firm in the face of adversity. Her resilience has inspired countless others to fight for their own right to live authentically, without fear of rejection or discrimination.

In interviews, Karla often speaks about the joy she finds in knowing that her work has made a positive impact on people's lives. The messages of support she receives from fans—many of whom are fellow members of the LGBTQ+ community—reinforce her belief that resilience is not just about survival but about thriving in a world that may not always understand you.

As she continues to break new ground and take on increasingly significant roles, Gascón's legacy will remain a beacon of hope for generations to come. Her resilience is not just an internal quality but a call to action for others to stand tall in their own lives. She has proven that no matter what obstacles life throws your way, the strength to overcome them can be found within—and that the power to shape your own destiny lies in your hands.

In the end, Karla Sofía Gascón's legacy is one of courage, resilience, and groundbreaking achievement. She has shown the world that no barrier is insurmountable, no dream too big, and that the path to success is paved not just with talent but with the unwavering belief in oneself.

Through her story, she continues to inspire and empower not just trans actors but all individuals striving to live authentically, proving that true strength lies in the courage to be who you are, unapologetically.

CONCLUSION

A Journey of Courage, Identity, and Redemption

Karla Sofía Gascón's remarkable journey from a young girl grappling with the complexities of identity under a dictatorial regime to a celebrated actress and groundbreaking advocate represents the essence of courage, resilience, and the power of authenticity.

Her path has not only shaped her career but also made an indelible mark on the global cultural landscape, where her performance in "Emilia Pérez" stands as a powerful symbol of transformation and redemption. This chapter reflects on the profound significance of Gascón's legacy, the cultural impact of "Emilia Pérez," and the enduring power of living authentically.

A Legacy of Courage and Transformation

Karla Sofía Gascón's legacy is one of courage in the face of adversity—a theme that runs through both her personal life and her work. From the moment she made the brave decision to transition and pursue her dreams of acting, Gascón defied societal expectations and overcame immense personal and professional challenges. Her decision to remain true to herself, despite the significant risks to her career and mental health, speaks volumes about her inner strength and determination.

Her legacy is not just defined by her accolades or the history she is making as a potential Oscar contender, but by the enduring message she imparts to the world: that one's true self, however difficult the journey, is always worth fighting for. Through her, we learn that the most transformative and redemptive journeys are often the ones that are most difficult and painful, yet they are the ones that define us the most.

Gascón's decision to act in roles that challenge her and the way people perceive gender shows that her work is not just about self-expression but about opening doors for others. Every part she plays and every project she takes on is another step in dismantling the narrow confines of traditional Hollywood storytelling and advocating for broader, more diverse representations of the human experience. Her legacy will continue to echo through the next generation of actors, activists, and dreamers, serving as a beacon of possibility and hope.

The Cultural Impact of "Emilia Pérez"

The release of "Emilia Pérez" marked a significant cultural moment. The film's themes of gender transition, redemption, and personal transformation intersected with the global movement for LGBTQ+ rights, creating a narrative that was not only timely but universally resonant. "Emilia Pérez" is more than just a film; it is a conversation starter, a bridge between cultures, and a reflection of societal changes that are unfolding in real time.

For the Latinx community, the film was a revolutionary moment—an opportunity to see a powerful, complex, and vulnerable trans woman portrayed by a trans actress, who has lived the experiences she is bringing to the screen. The film opened a space for Latinx audiences, both in Latin America and beyond, to engage with stories that are often sidelined or ignored by mainstream media. Karla Sofía Gascón's performance is not just a testament to her talent but also to the need for greater visibility and representation in storytelling.

For trans communities, "Emilia Pérez" offers a powerful reflection of their struggles and triumphs. The character of Emilia represents a trans woman's desire to escape a brutal past while seeking to create a meaningful future—a universal theme for anyone who has ever sought redemption or a second chance. As Gascón herself has pointed out, this film allows for a profound connectedness with audiences, many of whom see their own experiences reflected in Emilia's journey.

The cultural significance of "Emilia Pérez" extends far beyond the screen. The film's success, both critically and with audiences, is a victory for trans visibility in mainstream cinema. Gascón's portrayal of Emilia is more than just acting—it's a call to dismantle the barriers that prevent trans stories from being told with depth, authenticity, and respect. By doing so, *Emilia Pérez* becomes a piece of art that both entertains and educates, paving the way for more inclusive and representative films to follow.

The Enduring Power of Authenticity

At the heart of Karla Sofía Gascón's story is the enduring power of authenticity. Throughout her life, she has faced obstacles and judgments, but she has consistently remained steadfast in her commitment to living as her true self. Whether in her personal journey toward transitioning or her decision to embrace roles that reflect her identity, Gascón's authenticity has been a guiding force.

The success of "Emilia Pérez" is not only a recognition of her immense talent as an actress but a celebration of the authenticity that she brings to every role she plays. By choosing to live authentically, she has shown that the power of being true to oneself cannot be overstated. In a world that often demands conformity, her journey is a testament to the freedom and fulfillment that comes with embracing one's true identity.

This authenticity extends beyond the screen. Gascón's willingness to speak openly about her transition, the challenges she has faced, and the joy she finds in living her truth provides a roadmap for others to follow. Her story is an example of how embracing one's identity can lead to profound self-discovery and acceptance, and it encourages others to stand proudly in their own truth, regardless of external pressures.

As she continues to advocate for transgender visibility and acceptance, Gascón's message remains clear: there is power in living authentically, and when we are able to do so, we become stronger, more resilient, and more capable of making a lasting impact on the world. Her life and career remind us that authenticity is not only a personal victory—it is a force that can change the world.

A Final Reflection on Redemption

In many ways, Karla Sofía Gascón's life is a story of redemption. It is a redemption that comes not from external validation or awards, but from the process of self-acceptance and transformation. Her journey is a testament to the fact that redemption is not about erasing the past but about embracing it and using it as a stepping stone to build a better future.

The themes of "Emilia Pérez" echo this very concept of redemption—Emilia's quest to leave behind a violent and troubled past to create something positive and meaningful. Gascón, through her portrayal of this character, has found a form of redemption that is both personal and professional, one that serves as an inspiration for those who are also looking to overcome their own struggles.

As she looks toward the future, Karla Sofía Gascón's legacy is assured. Her impact on the entertainment industry, on the LGBTQ+ community, and on the wider world is undeniable. And while her career is just beginning to reach its peak, her influence will be felt for generations to come. She has proven that no matter the obstacles, no matter the pain or the doubts, it is possible to live authentically, to pursue one's dreams, and to leave an indelible mark on the world.

Karla Sofía Gascón's journey is a reminder to all of us that courage, identity, and redemption are not just abstract concepts—they are powerful forces that can shape our lives and our world for the better.

THANKS FOR READING!!!

www.ingramcontent.com/pod-product-compliance
Lightning Source LLC
LaVergne TN
LVHW021235150125
801343LV00001B/179

* 9 7 9 8 3 3 0 5 8 3 5 8 4 *